This book
belongs to

Nikki Smithurst.

First Science Encyclopedia

Written by

Kate Scarborough and Philippa Moyle

Illustrated by

Teresa Foster

Contents

zigzag

What is science?

Look at the things around you. Do you know what they are made from and how they work? The people who try to answer these questions are called scientists. They study the world around them and try to understand it. This is science.

In this book, you will find eight different scientists who study their own science. They introduce themselves on this page.

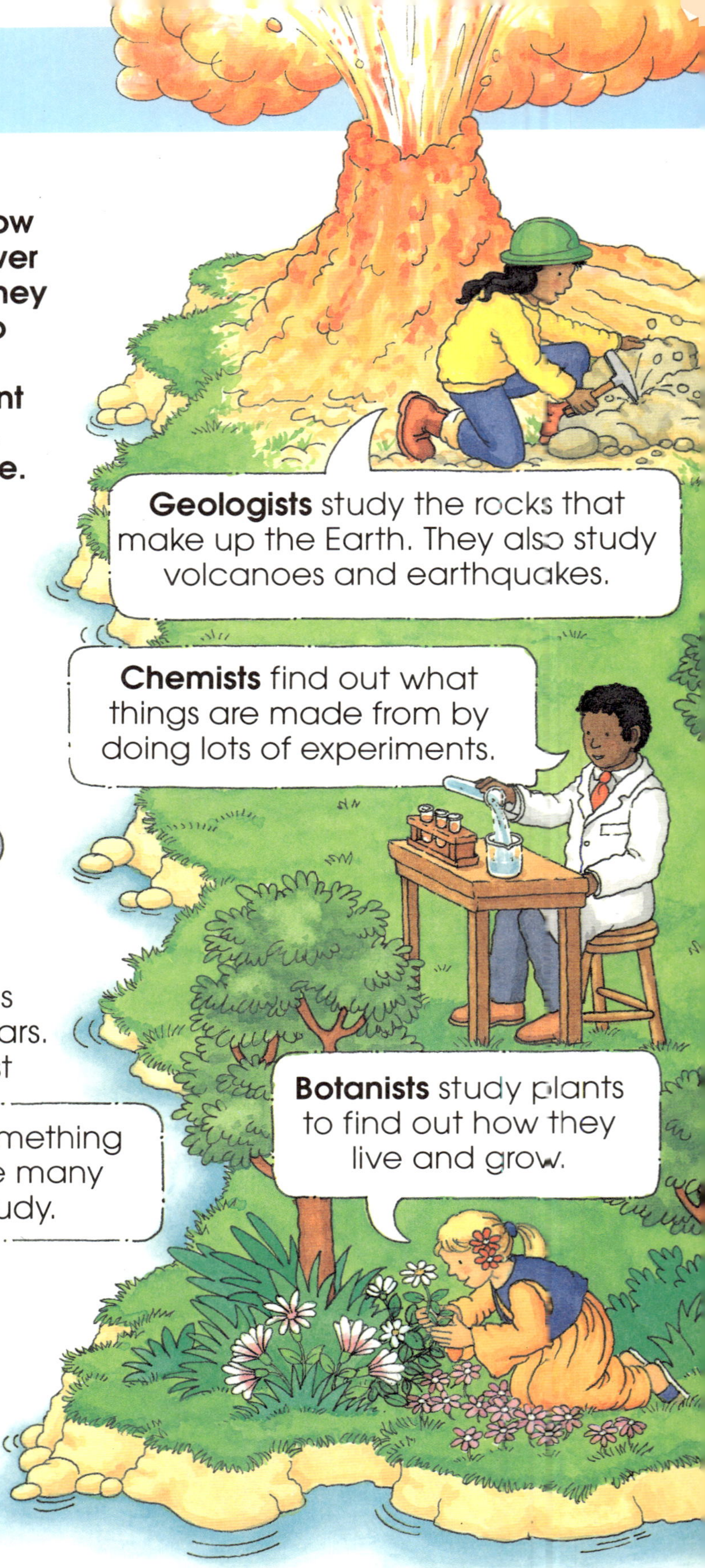

Scientists have made lots of discoveries and invented many things over the years. In 1879 Thomas Edison invented the first electric lamp.

Thomas Edison

Famous scientists

Aristotle was one of the earliest scientists. He lived in Greece around 2,500 years ago.

Galileo Galilei (1564-1642) was an Italian scientist. He is famous for saying that the Earth goes round the Sun instead of the Sun goes round the Earth.

Sir Isaac Newton (1642-1727) discovered that there are various laws for all kinds of movement.

Albert Einstein (1879-1955) was a brilliant physicist who worked on the science of time and light.

How do scientists work?

Scientists do tests, called experiments, to find out what things are made from and how they work. Many scientists do their experiments inside laboratories, using expensive equipment. However, you can be a scientist and do lots of experiments at home!

Microscopes

Many scientists use microscopes to help them with their work. Microscopes make tiny objects look much bigger, so that you can see them more clearly.

Satellites

Satellites are spacecraft that circle around a planet in space. Satellites have many different uses. Astronomers and meteorologists use them for their scientific work.

Computers

Computers are very useful to scientists. They can store lots of information which can be called up on to the screen at any time. Computers can be programmed to do many things.

How your body works

There are 220 bones in an adult's body.

Your body can do hundreds of things at the same time. You breathe and grow without thinking about it. How does this happen? The answers lie underneath your skin!

Body records

The tallest person ever was Robert Pershing Wadlow who was 272 cm tall.

The shortest person ever was Pauline Musters who was 61 cm tall.

The heaviest person ever was Jon Brower Minnoch who weighed more than 363 kg when he died.

The oldest person ever was Shigechiuyo Izumi from Japan who lived to 120.

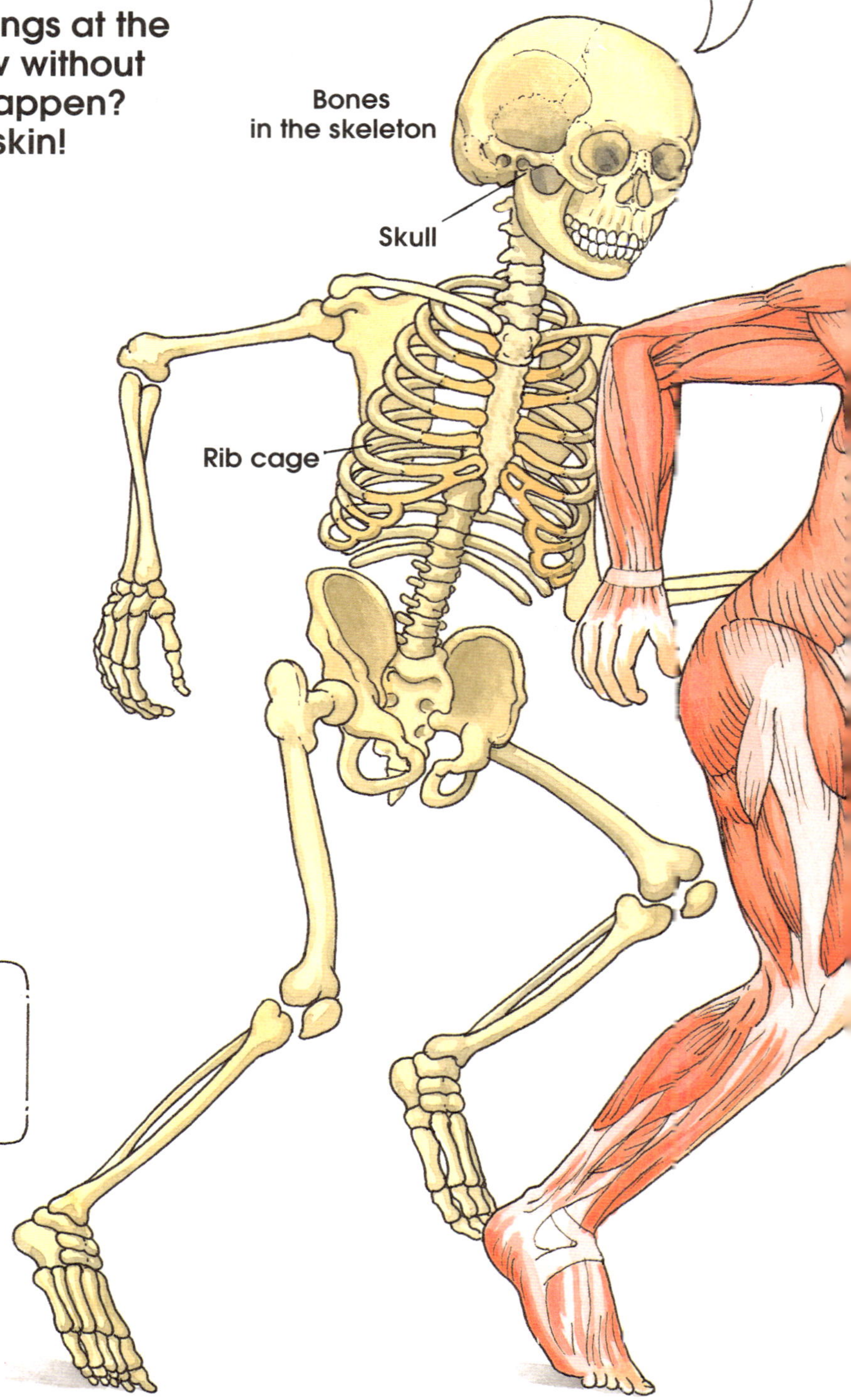

As you get older you grow taller. You stop growing when you reach your full height.

Measure one of your parents, too. Are they still growing?

Measure yourself once a month to see if you have grown.

The skeleton

The skeleton gives your body its shape. It is made up of different bones. Bones are made of a strong, hard substance.

Muscles

Muscles hold your bones in the right position. They also pull on the bones to make your body move.

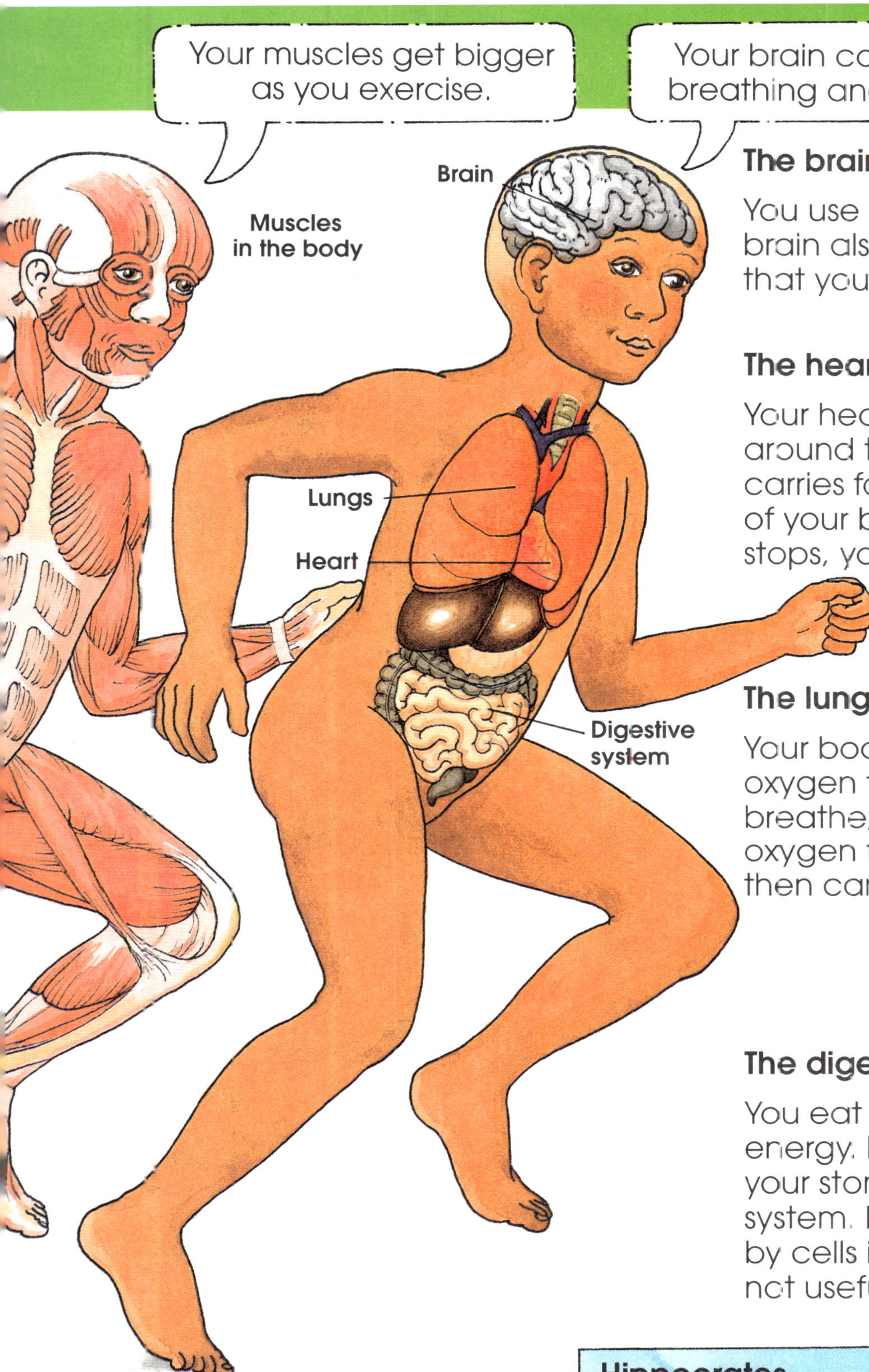

The brain

You use your brain to think. Your brain also controls everything that your body does.

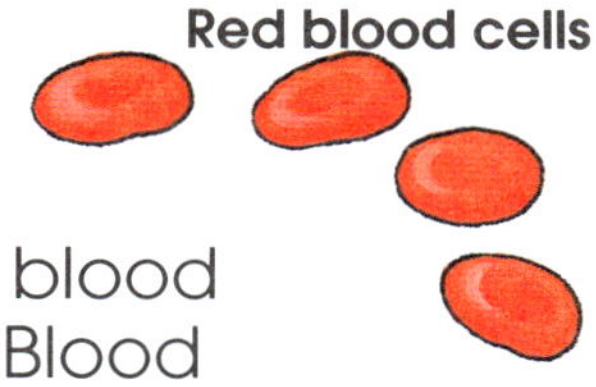

The heart

Your heart pumps blood around the body. Blood carries food to every part of your body. If your heart stops, you could die.

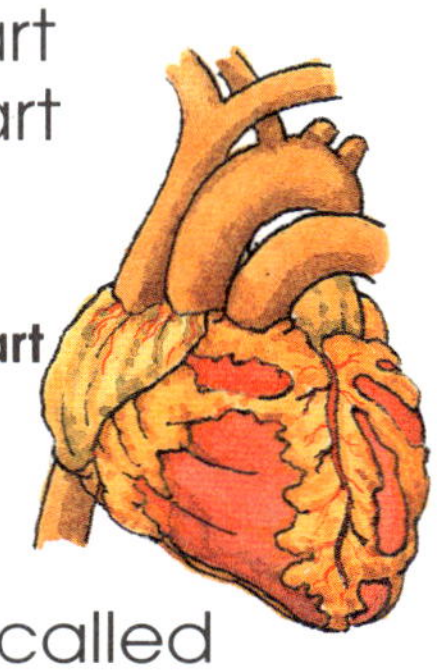

The lungs

Your body needs a gas called oxygen to live. When you breathe, your lungs take in oxygen from the air. The blood then carries it round your body.

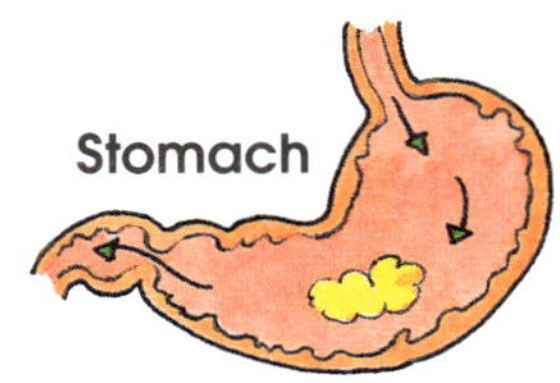

The digestive system

You eat food to give your body energy. Food is broken down in your stomach and digestive system. It is changed to energy by cells in your body. Whatever is not useful is got rid of as waste.

Skin

Skin is a waterproof layer that covers the whole of your body. It keeps out dirt and germs. It also feels things that you touch.

Hippocrates

Hippocrates is known as the 'Father of Medicine'. He was born on Kos, a Greek island, between about 500-400 BC. He travelled around Greece and the Middle East, teaching the people he met to look at the human body from a scientific point of view.

The body's senses

You use your skin to touch, your eyes to see, your ears to hear, your nose to smell and your tongue to taste. These are the five senses. Your senses send messages to your brain, telling it what is going on around you.

Seeing

To see an object clearly, you have to focus your eyes on it by looking directly at it.

Touching

You touch things with your skin which is very sensitive.

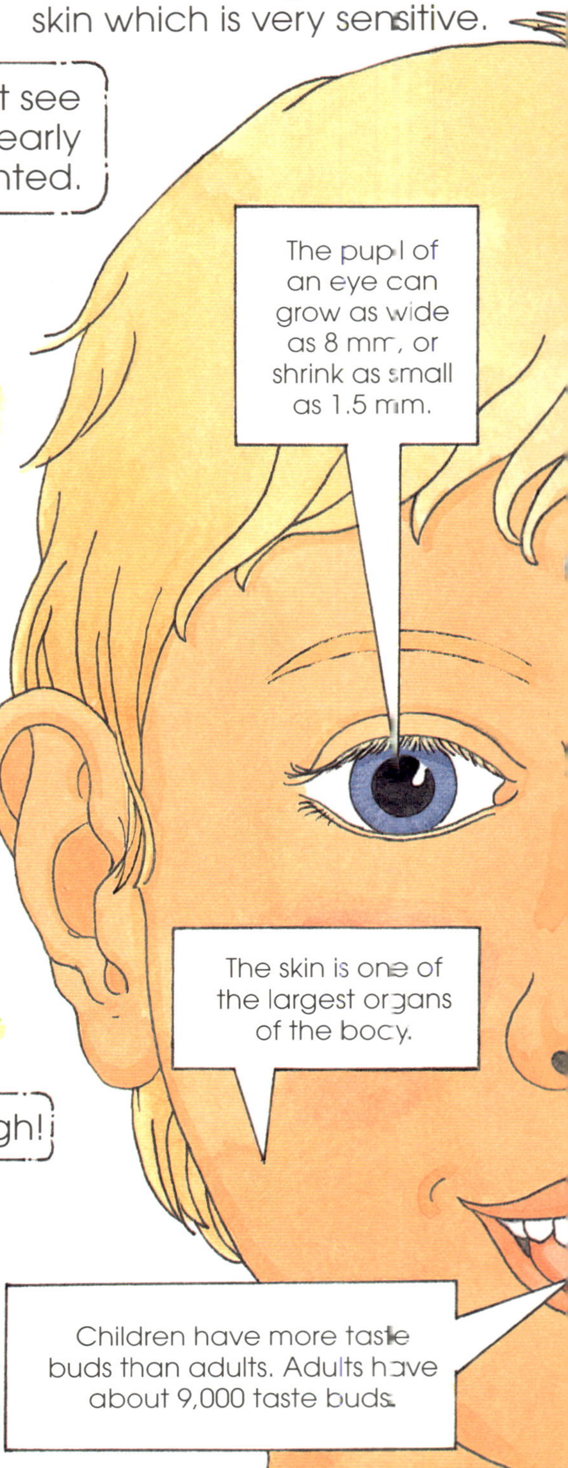

Hearing

Your ears can hear many different sounds. Apart from your outer ear, the rest of your ear is inside your head (see page 26 for a diagram of the ear).

Smelling

You smell things with your nose. Some smells are pleasant, but others are not.

Human senses are not as good as the senses of other animals.

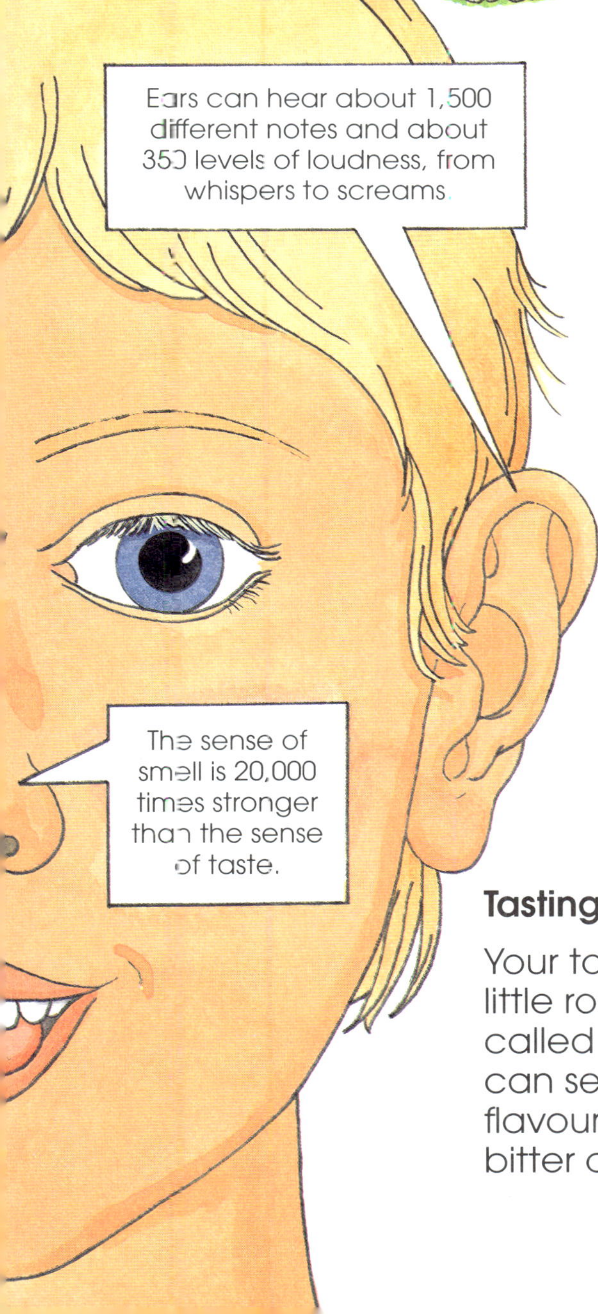

Try it yourself!

Sight

Your eyes can trick you. Look at this pattern. It looks like a spiral but, in fact, it is a pattern of circles that don't touch each other.

Taste and smell

When you have a blocked nose and can't smell, you often find that you can't taste food. Try this experiment to see how taste and smell are linked.
Blindfold a friend and give them four fruit yoghurts to eat. They should be able to tell the difference between the yoghurts. Then ask them to do the same thing while holding their nose. Can they tell which yoghurt is which?

Tasting

Your tongue has many little round buds on it, called taste buds. They can sense four main flavours - sweet, sour, bitter and salty.

The world of animals

Scientists who study animals are called zoologists. There are about a million known types of animal in the world. There may be more that have not yet been discovered.
There are two large groups of animals. Animals that have a backbone are called vertebrates. They include mammals, birds, reptiles, fish and amphibians. Animals that do not have a backbone are called invertebrates. They include arthropods, molluscs, annelids and other animals, such as jellyfish and starfish.

Mammals

The bodies of mammals are covered in hair. Female mammals feed their babies on their own milk. Human beings, dogs, tigers, whales and bats are all mammals.

Amphibians

Amphibians live half in water and half on the land. They usually lay their eggs in the water. Frogs and newts are amphibians.

Fish

Fish live in water. They are covered in scales, have fins and lay eggs. Sharks and salmon are fish.

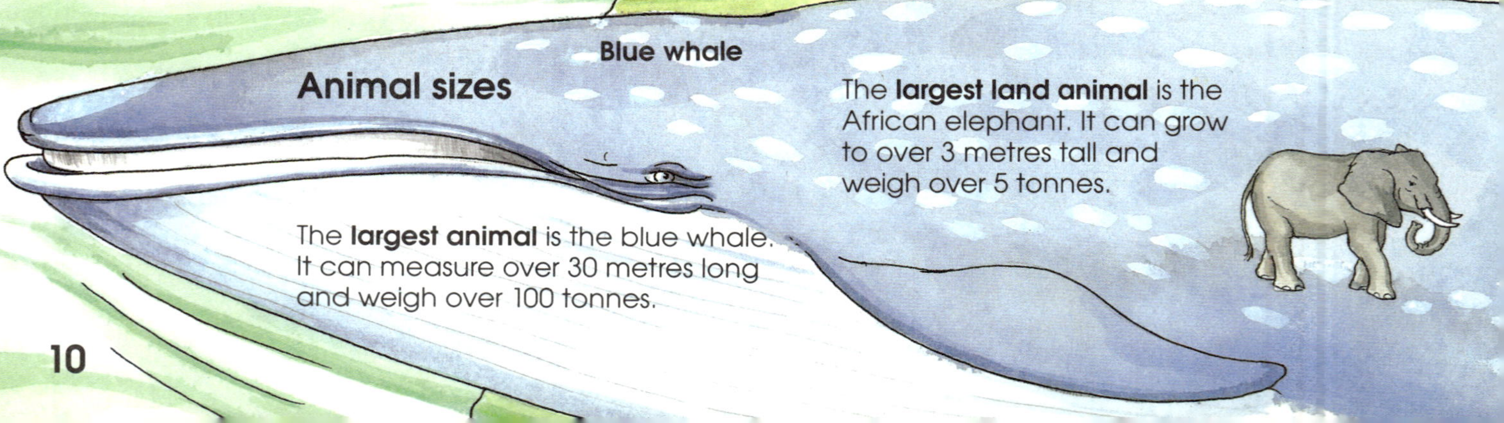

Animal sizes

The **largest land animal** is the African elephant. It can grow to over 3 metres tall and weigh over 5 tonnes.

The **largest animal** is the blue whale. It can measure over 30 metres long and weigh over 100 tonnes.

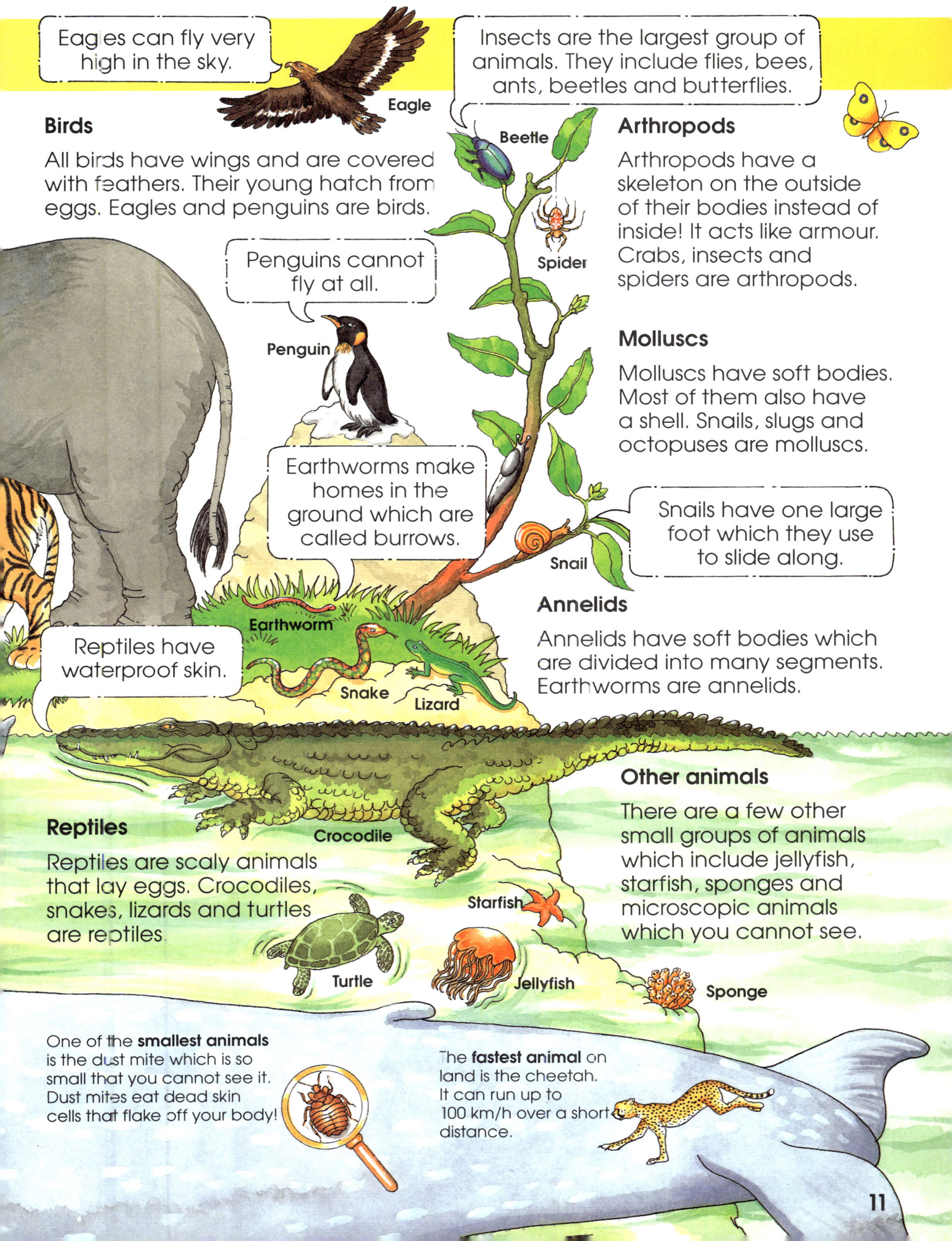

Birds

All birds have wings and are covered with feathers. Their young hatch from eggs. Eagles and penguins are birds.

Arthropods

Arthropods have a skeleton on the outside of their bodies instead of inside! It acts like armour. Crabs, insects and spiders are arthropods.

Molluscs

Molluscs have soft bodies. Most of them also have a shell. Snails, slugs and octopuses are molluscs.

Annelids

Annelids have soft bodies which are divided into many segments. Earthworms are annelids.

Reptiles

Reptiles are scaly animals that lay eggs. Crocodiles, snakes, lizards and turtles are reptiles.

Other animals

There are a few other small groups of animals which include jellyfish, starfish, sponges and microscopic animals which you cannot see.

One of the **smallest animals** is the dust mite which is so small that you cannot see it. Dust mites eat dead skin cells that flake off your body!

The **fastest animal** on land is the cheetah. It can run up to 100 km/h over a short distance.

How animals live

Around the world there are hot, dry deserts, freezing cold regions, forests, oceans, lakes, rivers, mountains and cities. Animals live in all of these different places.

Habitats

Animals live in different habitats. Polar bears live in the freezing Arctic. Kangaroo rats live in hot deserts in North America.

Caring for the young

Many animals build homes to protect their young from danger. Rabbits make burrows in the ground, while birds make nests in trees. Ants build mounds called anthills.

Animals in danger

Over the millions of years that animals have existed, many kinds have disappeared completely. They have become extinct. Dinosaurs became extinct over 75 million years ago. We know they existed because we have found their bones deep in the ground. Today, there are many kinds of animals that could soon become extinct. There are only about 200 giant pandas and about 50 whooping cranes left in the world.

Finding food

A few animals have amazing senses which help them to find food. Vultures have excellent eyesight which allows them to see something to eat from a great height.

Some animals eat only meat. They are called carnivores.

Some animals eat only plants. They are called herbivores.

Charles Darwin

Charles Darwin (1809-1882) is one of the most famous people to study animals. He travelled all over the world studying animals in their natural habitats. He believed that all living things are constantly changing, or evolving, over long periods of time to fit better into their surroundings. This changing is called evolution.

Hiding

Animals hide themselves by blending their bodies into the background. Leopards hide in tall grasses while they hunt for animals to eat. Grey tree frogs are covered in a pattern that looks like the bark of a tree, so that they will not be seen and eaten.

Animals that hunt other animals are called predators.

Showing off

Some animals like to show off to attract a mate. Male peacocks display their fabulous tails. Humpbacked whales sing songs that can be heard hundreds of kilometres away.

Animals that are hunted are called prey.

The world of plants

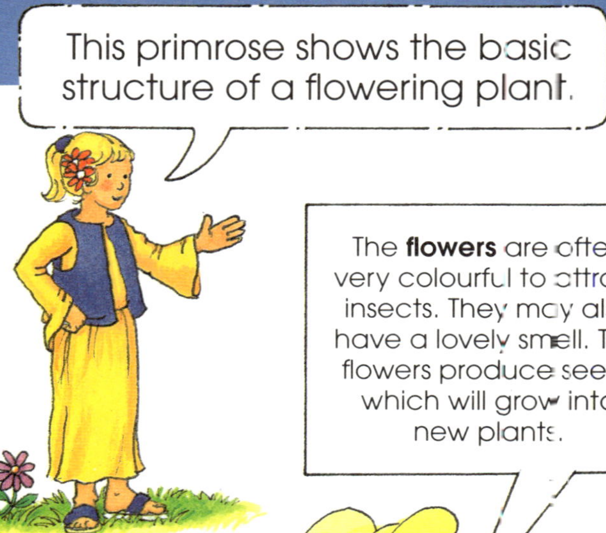

There are about 450,000 kinds of plants in the world. Scientists that study plants are called botanists. Botanists divide plants into groups in the same way as zoologists divide animals into groups. Botanists have discovered that there are some plants that have flowers and other plants that don't have flowers.

Flowering plants

Over half of the 450,000 kinds of plants in the world produce flowers. Flowers are important to plants as they produce seeds which grow into other plants. Flowering plants can be very large, like a horse chestnut tree. This produces large, shiny, brown seeds called conkers.

Carl Linnaeus

Carl Linnaeus (1707-1778) was a Swedish botanist who invented a way of dividing plants into groups. He named nearly 8,000 kinds of plants and over 4,000 kinds of animals as well. He gave each one two names which were in Latin.

Conifers

Conifers are trees that produce their seeds in cones. Their leaves are shaped like needles. Pine trees are conifers.

Algae

Most algae live in water. Some of them are tiny plants that you can't see. Others are large seaweeds.

Ferns and mosses

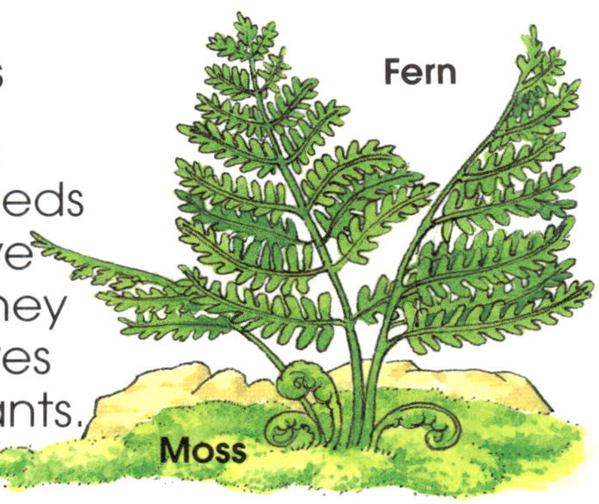

Ferns and mosses don't produce seeds as they don't have flowers. Instead they produce tiny spores that grow into plants.

Plant facts

The leaves of a cactus are shaped like needles and are very sharp.

The flower of a bee orchid looks just like a female bee.

A clover has three rounded leaves. If you find one with four leaves, it is meant to be lucky.

Bluebells have flowers that look upside down and the petals grow stuck together.

How plants live

As a year passes you will see changes in the plants around you. Plants grow quickly or slowly depending on whether it is spring, summer or autumn. In winter, plants hardly grow at all.

Short-living plants

Marigolds are annuals

Some plants only live for one year. They are called annuals. Annuals grow from seeds in the spring. They flower in the summer, produce seeds and then die.

Long-living plants

Some plants live for many years. Trees are a good example of this. Each year they grow bigger. After a tree has been cut down, you can tell how old it was by counting the rings in the trunk.

In **spring**, leaves and apple blossom appear on the branches.

In **winter**, the leaves have gone and the branches are bare.

An apple tree during one year

Try these experiments to show that plants need light and water to grow.

Try it yourself!

To show that plants need water

Place a bean seed in a glass jar full of damp cotton wool. Put another bean seed in a jar full of dry cotton wool. Keep watering the jar with damp cotton wool inside but leave the other jar alone.

In **summer**, green leaves cover the branches.

In **autumn**, ripe apples hang from the branches and the leaves start to fall.

Large flowers

The rafflesia plant in the Malaysian rainforest produces the largest and smelliest flowers in the world. They can measure up to 91 cm across and weigh up to 7 kilograms.

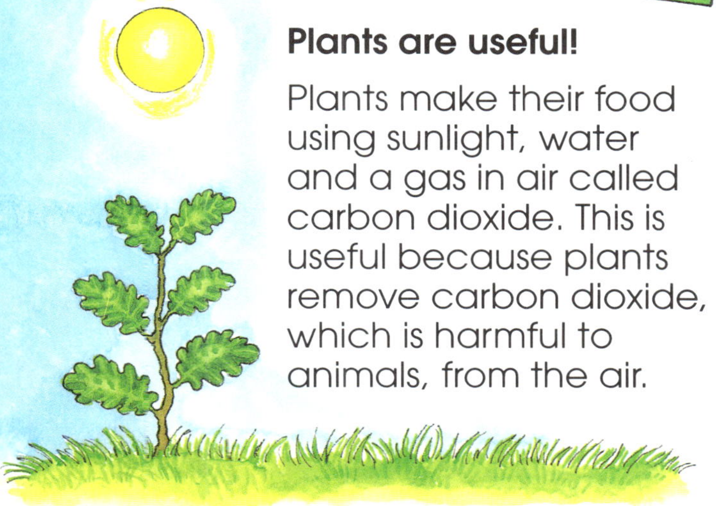

Plants are useful!

Plants make their food using sunlight, water and a gas in air called carbon dioxide. This is useful because plants remove carbon dioxide, which is harmful to animals, from the air.

Food, medicines and clothes

Plants are very useful to people. People eat plants, such as vegetables, and make medicines from herbs. They also use plants to make clothes. Many clothes are made from cotton which comes from the cotton plant.

Vegetables

Cotton

After four days, look at the seeds. The bean seed in the damp cotton wool should have grown a root. The one in the dry cotton wool should not have changed at all.

To show that plants need light

Cover both sides of a leaf on a green plant with dark paper. After a couple of days, take off the paper. You should find that the leaf has changed colour from green to yellow.

What are things made of?

If you look around you, you can see objects everywhere. Outside, there are trees, cars, buildings, sky and clouds. Inside, there are objects like chairs, carpets and windows. What are they all made of? Scientists who study what things are made of are called chemists.

Metal

Metal is a solid. When you touch metal it feels cold. You can polish it so that it becomes shiny. You can also paint it. Knives, forks and saucepans can be made of metal.

Wood

Wood is a solid. When you touch wood it does not usually feel cold. Chairs, tables, doors, paper and pencils can be made of wood.

Glass

Glass is a solid that can easily be broken. Windows, mirrors and light bulbs can be made of glass.

Plastic

Plastic is a solid that is made by chemists. Some plastics are very hard and others are bendy. Bowls and bottles can be made of plastic.

Alchemists

Modern chemistry probably began in the seventeenth century. Before this time, the people who studied how things were made were called alchemists. During their experiments, they found that they could change things from one form to another. People believed that any metal could be turned into gold. A lot of people tried to do this, but no one managed it!

Solids cannot change their shape.

Liquids can easily change their shape.

Gases do not have a definite shape.

Solids

You can move a television, but you can't change its shape. A television is a solid.

Liquids

You can pour water from a jug, which is one shape, into a glass, which is another shape. Water is a liquid.

Gases

The water vapour rising from boiling water is light and fills the room. It is a gas.

Water

Water is the most common liquid. Many other liquids, such as tea, orange juice and milk, are mostly made of water.

Oil

Oil is a liquid that can be used for cooking. It is thicker than water. If you pour oil and water into a cup, they do not mix.

Air

You may think that the space around you is empty. In fact it is filled with air. This is made from several different gases which you cannot see. One of these gases is carbon dioxide, which makes the bubbles in fizzy drinks.

Try it yourself!

Try this experiment to show that air is made of something.

Turn a glass upside down and push it down into a washing-up bowl full of water. You will find that the glass doesn't fill up with water. Turn the glass to one side and bubbles will come out from it. These are bubbles of air.

Hot and cold

You know when the weather is hot because you can wear a T-shirt without feeling cold. You can find out how hot or cold it is by using a thermometer to measure the temperature of the air.

Temperature

Temperature is measured in degrees. You can measure it in degrees Celsius (°C) or degrees Fahrenheit (°F). A thermometer shows both the Celsius scale and the Fahrenheit scale.

Hot air balloons

Air is made up of a mixture of gases. When gases are heated they take up more space and become lighter - less dense. This happens because the particles of gas move faster and spread out.

Try it yourself!

Some solids allow heat to pass along them to another object. If a solid warms up quickly it is a good carrier of heat. Try this experiment to see which solid is best at carrying heat.

1 Find three spoons - one metal, one wooden and one plastic.

2 Put a tiny spot of butter on the end of each spoon and stick a frozen pea on to the butter.

Freezing water

When water freezes it turns into a solid called ice. Lollies are made of ice.

Boiling water

When water boils it turns into a gas called water vapour.

When the air in a large balloon is heated, the particles of gas spread out and fill the balloon. The air inside the balloon is now less dense than the air outside it, so the balloon rises into the sky.

Solids can melt!

Most solids will turn into liquids if they are heated to a high enough temperature. For example, a solid wax candle will melt into liquid wax when it is heated.

3 Put all the spoons into a mug of hot water.

Each pea will fall off when the spoon it is on becomes warm enough to melt the butter. Watch to see which pea falls off first. The first pea to fall will be the one that was on the spoon that was best at carrying heat.

Water

Plants and animals, including human beings, depend on water to keep them alive. Living creatures contain a lot of water. Nearly two-thirds of your body is made up of water.

How does a ship float?

Objects that are less dense, or lighter, than water can float. A heavy ship can float because its weight is less than the weight of water it pushes aside. You can see how this works below.

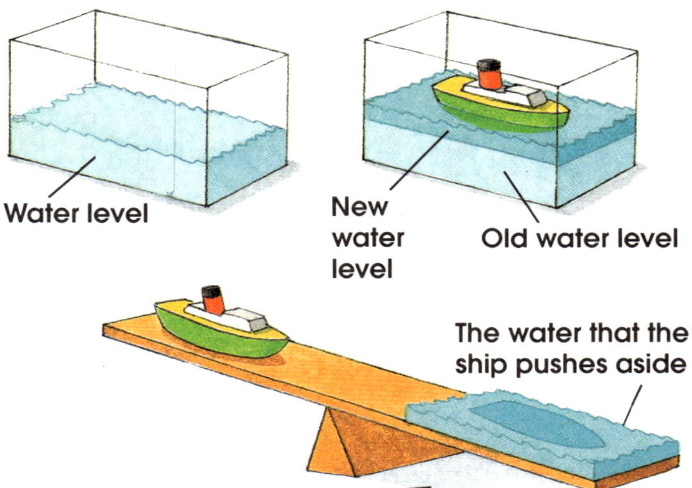

Try it yourself!

Fill a bowl with water. Take two lumps of modelling clay. Leave one as a lump, and make the other into the shape of a boat. Drop both of them into the bowl and watch what happens.

Water turns into a gas

When you leave wet clothes on a washing line, they slowly become dry. This is because the liquid water in the clothes becomes warm and turns into a gas, water vapour. This process is called evaporation - the liquid water evaporates into water vapour.

Exploring the sea

In 1690, Sir Edmund Halley invented a diving bell. This was a bell-shaped container which was used to explore underwater. Two people sat inside the bell. A third person swam outside collecting treasure from a sunken wreck.

Icebergs

When water freezes it turns into solid ice. Icebergs are huge pieces of ice that float in very cold water. Areas near the North and South Poles have icebergs.

A gas turns into water

When you run a bath of hot water the window mists up.

This process is called condensation - the water vapour condenses into liquid water.

Try it yourself!

Make your own icebergs by putting some ice cubes from the freezer into a glass of water. Do they float or sink? They should float. This shows that ice is less dense than water.

Light

The Sun gives us light. If there was no light from the Sun, there would be no life on Earth because plants and animals need light in order to live.

Day and night

We have day and night because the Earth spins round, making one whole spin in 24 hours. When the country you live in faces the Sun you have daylight, and when it faces away from the Sun you have darkness.

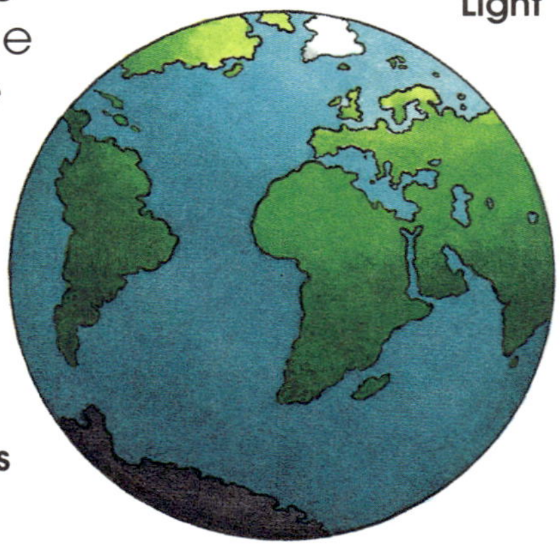

Shadows

If you are outside on a sunny day you will see your shadow on the ground. There is a shadow because light cannot travel through you. If you look around you will see that other objects have shadows, too. Light cannot travel through anything that isn't see-through.

Reflection

You can only see things when there is light. When you look at an object, such as a tree, what you really see is light from the Sun reflected off the tree.

Colours

Light allows you to see the colour of the things around you. When there isn't much light, they look grey.

Rainbows

Sunlight looks white but a rainbow shows that sunlight is made of different colours. A rainbow forms when white sunlight shines through raindrops and is broken into different colours. Together, these colours are called the spectrum.

Try it yourself!

Hold a page of this book in front of a mirror. You are looking at a reflection of the page. What has happened to the writing and pictures? Everything is back to front. When you look at your face in the mirror you see it back to front, too. This is because the mirror reflects back exactly what it sees.

Sound

Sit still for a moment and listen. What can you hear? You may hear people talking, a car driving past or an aeroplane flying overhead. These are all sounds.

Sound waves

If you drop a stone into still water, you will see waves travel out from it. Sound travels like this. When a sound is made, sound waves travel out from it. They are made by vibrating air particles. Vibrating means moving backwards and forwards very fast.

Sound waves hit the eardrum, making it vibrate. The eardrum is a piece of skin that stretches across the tube of the ear.

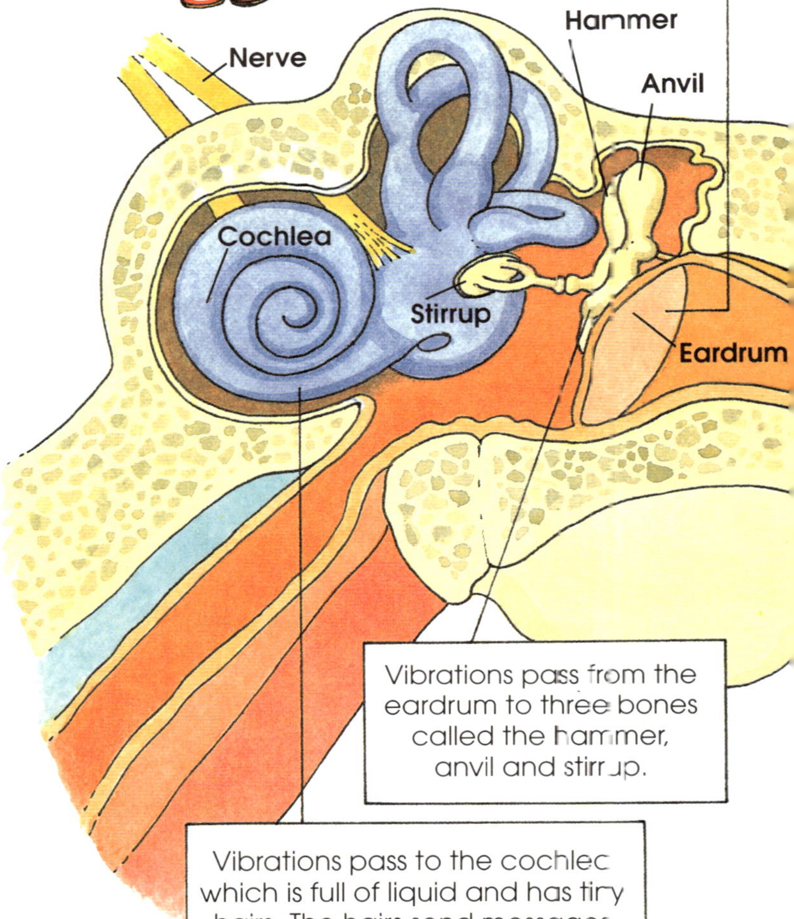

Vibrations pass from the eardrum to three bones called the hammer, anvil and stirrup.

Vibrations pass to the cochlea which is full of liquid and has tiny hairs. The hairs send messages along a nerve to your brain which understands the sound

Try it yourself!

Stretch some cling film over a round tin and sprinkle sugar on top of it. Hold a metal baking tray above the tin and bang the tray. You will see the sugar vibrate on top of the cling film. Sound waves travel through the air, making the cling film vibrate. This makes the sugar vibrate. The cling film behaves like your eardrum.

The ear

Most of your ear is inside your head. The outer ear is the only part you can see.

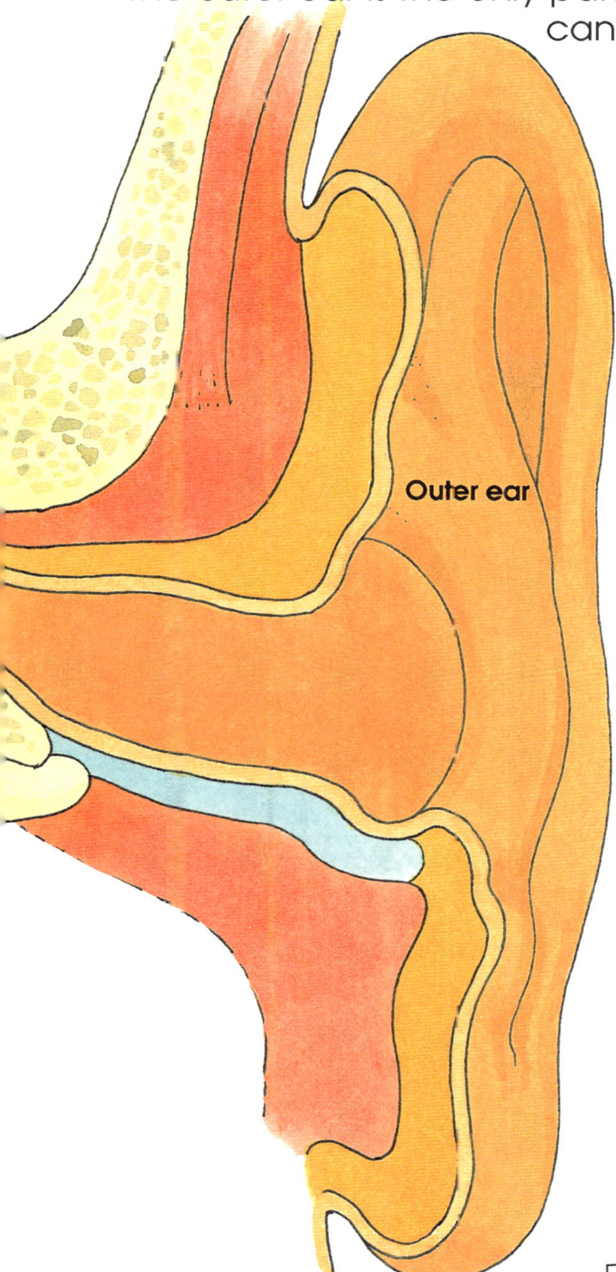

The speed of sound

Amerindians (native Americans) used to put one ear to the ground to listen for the sound of galloping horses. They did this because sound travels faster through solids, such as the ground, than through gases which make up the air.

Echoes

If you shout in a cave, you may hear the sound more than once. This is an echo. Usually, sound waves travel out from a sound and don't return. In this case, the sound waves bounce off the wall of the cave and return to you.

Try it yourself!

You can make your own telephone and talk to a friend! Tie a plastic cup to each end of a long piece of string. If you talk into one cup and your friend holds the other cup to their ear in another room, your friend should be able to hear you.

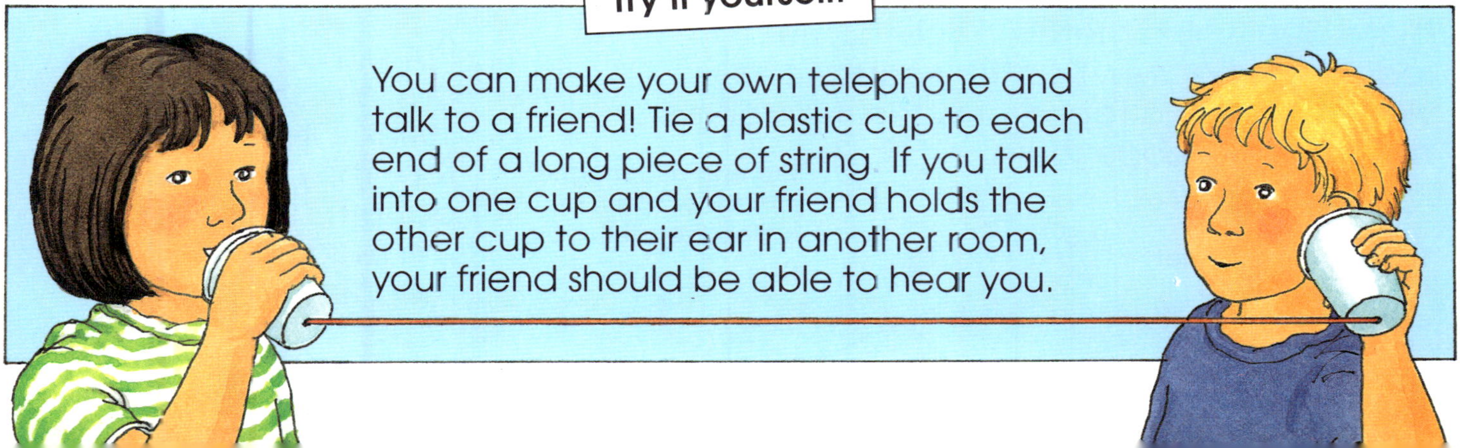

Forces

When you try to move something you use a force. A force is a push, a pull, a lift or a squash. A force can make something move or change its shape. You can see these forces in action, but there are invisible forces as well.

Magnets

Magnets have an invisible magnetic force called magnetism. Magnets pull some metals towards them. See which metals in your home react to a magnet. Don't try computers, video and audio tapes, or video recorders, as you will damage them.

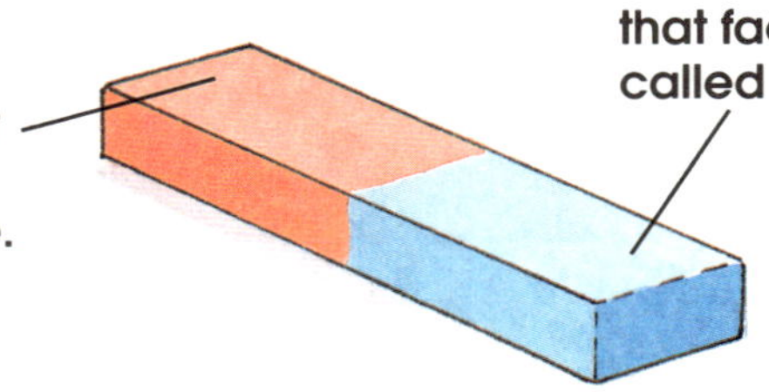

Try it yourself!

Put a magnet under a piece of card and sprinkle iron filings on top. They will make a pattern as they follow the magnet's lines of magnetic force.

Backwards and forwards

Whenever there is a force in one direction there is another force in the opposite direction. For example, when you stop pushing something forwards fast, you nearly fall over backwards!

Gravity

If you jump off a garden seat you won't fly up into the sky, but land on the ground. This is because the Earth has an invisible force that pulls you downwards. It is called gravity.

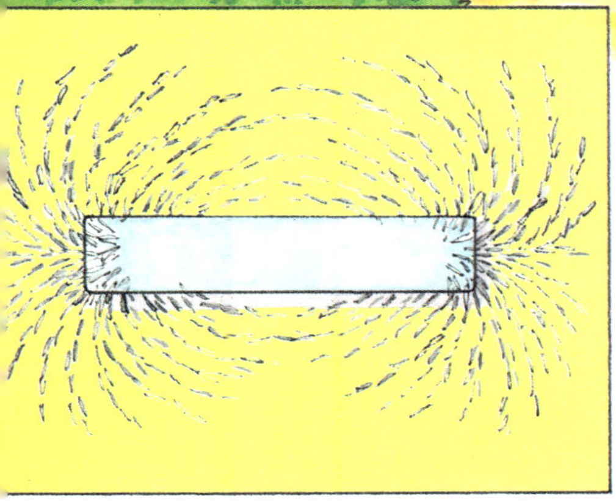

A compass

A type of rock called lodestone contains iron which is naturally magnetic. About 2,000 years ago, lodestone was used to make the first compass. The needle of a compass always points towards the north. Explorers use a compass to find out which direction they should travel in.

Making things move

It can sometimes be hard work making things move. However, there are simple ways to make it easier for you. Here are some of them:

Try it yourself!

Ask someone who is heavier than you to sit at one end of a see-saw. You cannot lift them if they sit at the other end, but if you ask them to sit nearer the middle, the pivot, you may find you can.

Levers

A lever is a simple machine that can make it easier to lift something. A see-saw is a type of lever. It is hard lifting a person heavier than yourself, but it may be possible to lift them into the air on a see-saw! A see-saw balances on a pivot.

Gears

Gears are wheels with teeth. They can be used to make one wheel turn more slowly or more quickly than another, or turn in a different direction. On a bicycle they are used to make cycling easier and faster, so that your legs don't have to turn the pedals as quickly as the wheels turn.

Inclined planes

An inclined plane is a slope. Inclined planes make it easier to move things. It would be very difficult to lift a wheelbarrow full of earth, but it is easier to push it up a slope.

Gears are used in many other machines as well as bicycles.

Moving in air

A bird makes flying through the air look so easy. But have you ever wondered how people and machines can move through the air? Studying shapes and air has made it possible for us to move in the air in all sorts of different ways.

To understand how things fly, you must know that air pushes objects from all directions. Air is therefore pushing upwards against anything that is falling. If a large, light object is falling, the air pushing against it can slow it down quite a lot.

Parachutes

A parachute has a large curved shape for the air to push against. That is why a parachute slows down as it falls. If you suddenly pull an umbrella down you can feel the air pushing up. But if you tried to use an umbrella as a parachute, you'd find that it would not work. This is because it is not big enough to support your weight.

Early flyers

The first successful human flights were made in hot air balloons (see page 20). Two French brothers, the Montgolfiers, sent a hot air balloon up into the sky in 1783. A hot air balloon is known as a lighter-than-air craft. The first heavier-than-air craft to fly was an aeroplane designed and flown by Orville Wright in 1903.

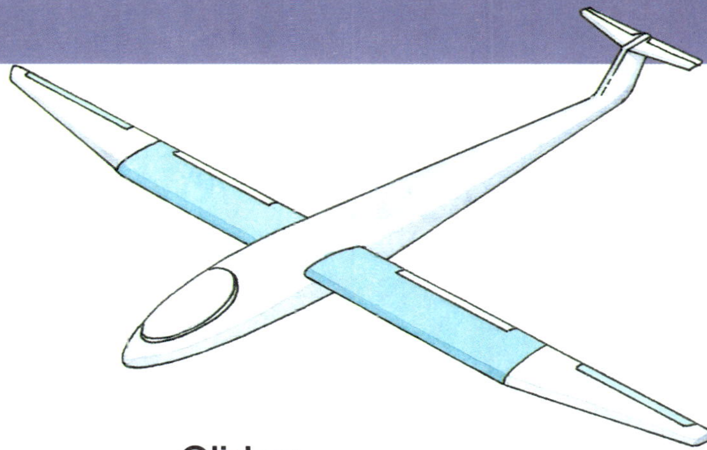

Gliders

Warm, moving air rising upwards can keep a glider in the air for a long time.

Kites

Kites are one of the earliest flying machines, dating back to 300 BC. They only work on windy days, when the moving air blows against the kite and pushes it up into the sky.

Try it yourself!

Air pushes against things. Hold a large piece of stiff card in front of you. Now try and run forwards as fast as you can. It's quite difficult isn't it? This is because the air is pushing against the card. If you hold the card the other way over your head and run, you will find it much easier.

The weather

What is the weather like at the moment? Is it sunny, cloudy, windy, raining or snowing? The weather can be any of these things. People who study the weather are called meteorologists.

When it is both sunny and raining you might see a rainbow.

Sunshine

Sunshine heats the ground and the sea. Some sea-water and water from lakes evaporates into the air - it becomes water vapour (see page 22).

Violent weather

A **storm** often has thunder and lightning as well as heavy rain and strong winds.

A **hurricane** is a violent storm with winds reaching more than 118 kilometres per hour.

A **cyclone** is a hurricane where the wind blows round in a circle. The winds can reach 250 kilometres per hour.

A **tornado** is a violently spinning whirlwind that travels across the surface of the land or sea.

If it is very windy you may get blown off your feet!

Wind

Wind is moving air. The wind can blow gently as a light breeze, or it can blow strongly as a gale.

Rain

The tiny water droplets in a cloud get bigger and bigger until they are so heavy that they fall to the ground as rain.

Clouds

Air containing water vapour rises high into the sky. The water vapour condenses into tiny droplets of water. Thousands of these droplets form a cloud.

Climates

If you look at the pattern of weather in one place over a period of time you will find out the place's climate. There are several different climates around the world. The study of climates is called climatology.

Snow

When it is very cold, the water droplets in the air freeze and fall to the ground as snow instead of rain.

The Earth

The Earth is shaped like a round ball. It is a planet that circles around the Sun in space. Seventy per cent of the surface of the Earth is water which is found in the seas and oceans. The people who study the Earth and how it is made are called geologists.

Soil

The top layer of the ground is soil. Soil is made of tiny bits of rock, rotting plants and animals. Plants and trees grow in the soil.

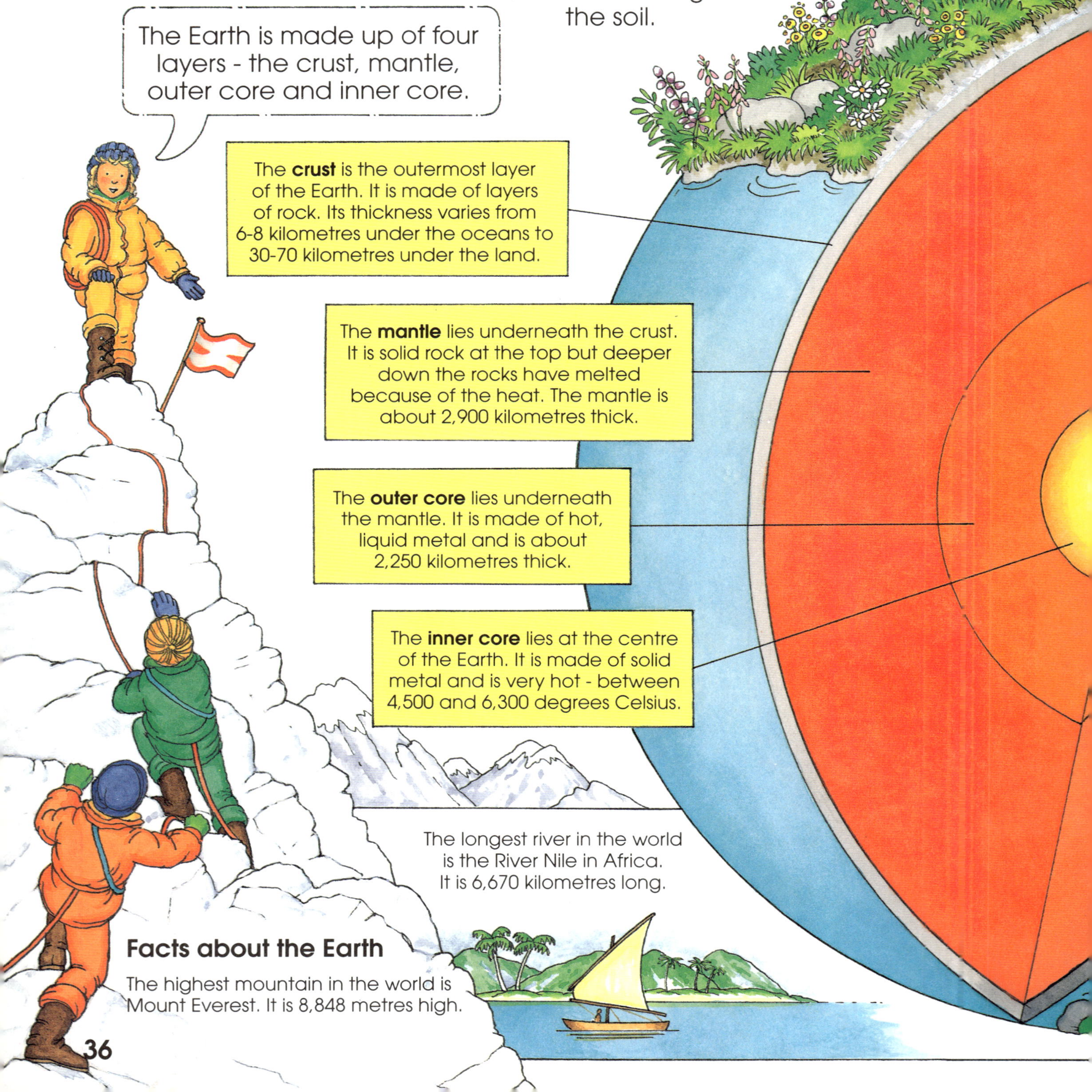

Facts about the Earth

The highest mountain in the world is Mount Everest. It is 8,848 metres high.

The longest river in the world is the River Nile in Africa. It is 6,670 kilometres long.

Rocks

Underneath the soil there are different types of rocks. Some are very hard, such as granite and marble, while others are crumbly such as shale and chalk.

Fossils

In some rocks you can find fossils of ancient plants and animals. Fossils show the shape of the hard parts of a creature that died thousands of years ago.

A changing landscape

The landscape of the Earth is always changing. For example, the waves of the sea wear away cliffs made of rock. This changes their shape so that the landscape looks different.

Volcanoes and earthquakes

Volcanoes and earthquakes change the landscape in a dramatic way. When a volcano erupts, molten rock called lava explodes into the air. As it cools, it forms a new landscape. Earthquakes make the ground shake, causing buildings to fall down. Whole towns can be destroyed by an earthquake.

The deepest part of an ocean is the Marianas Trench in the Pacific Ocean. It is 11,033 metres deep.

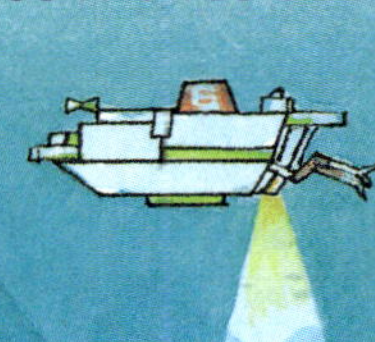

The biggest volcanic eruption took place at Tambora in Indonesia in 1815.

Space

If you look up into the sky on a clear night you will see the Moon and hundreds of twinkling stars. There are thousands of other stars and planets in space that are too far away for you to see. Scientists who study the night sky are called astronomers.

The universe

The whole of space is called the universe. It contains billions of galaxies, which are huge groups of stars, planets and other space bodies. Our galaxy is called the Milky Way. It contains 100,000 million stars!

The Sun

The Sun is a star. It is the nearest star to the Earth. The Sun gives the Earth its heat and light.

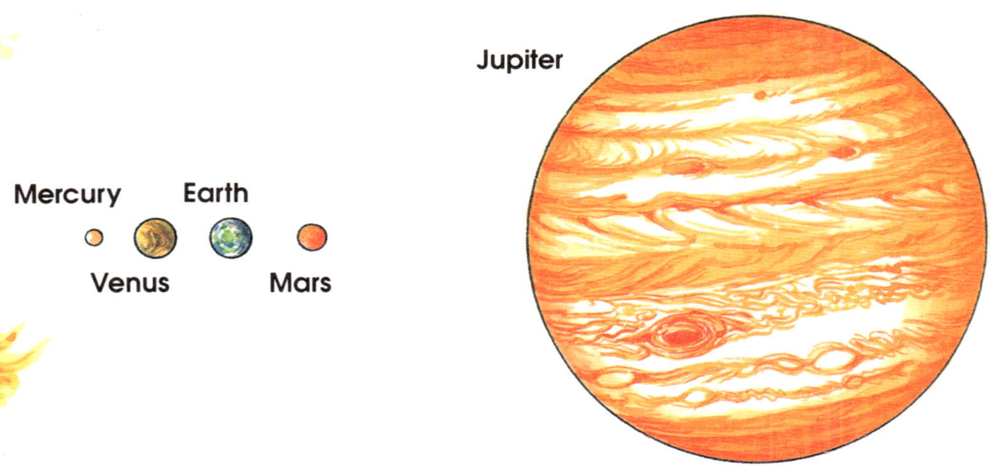

Exploring space

Astronomers use telescopes to look at the stars. They also send rockets, satellites and probes into space to take photographs of planets. Although we know a lot about the universe, there is still much more to discover.

If you imagine the Sun about the size of a beach ball, the Earth would be about the size of a pea!

Stars

When you look at the stars twinkling in the night sky they seem tiny because they are so far away in space. In fact, each star is a huge ball of gases that burns very brightly.

The Moon

Neil Armstrong

The Moon circles around the Earth. Neil Armstrong, an American, was the first person to step on to the Moon in 1969.

The planets

The Earth is a planet that circles around the Sun. There are eight other main planets in the Solar System called Mercury, Venus, Mars, Jupiter, Saturn, Uranus, Neptune and Pluto. In addition to these main planets there are other lumps of rock in space called minor planets.

The distances between the planets shown below are not exact.

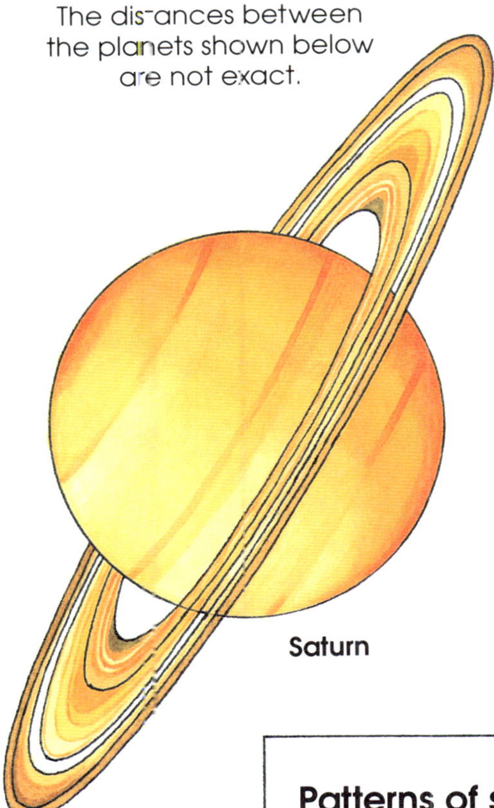

Saturn

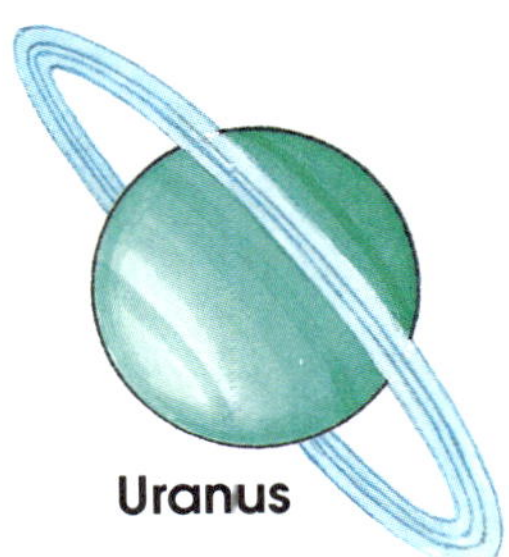

Uranus

Neptune

Pluto

Patterns of stars

Groups of stars make patterns in the night sky. These are called constellations. Ancient Greek astronomers gave these constellations names after their gods and myths. The constellation shown on the right is called Orion the hunter.

Index

This edition published 1998 by Zigzag Publishing, a division of Quadrillion Publishing Ltd., Godalming, Surrey, GU7 1XW.

Consultant: Lillian Wright has worked as a freelance Primary Science Consultant and Curriculum Adviser for Science.

Editor: Philippa Moyle
Designer: David Anstey
Cover design by Danny McBride and Nicky Chapman
Series concept: Tony Potter

8519 Printed in Singapore

ISBN 1-85833-877-8